Contents

) Bod___

Want to b___
fit and ___
Here's ___

t Two) Zitz

pots, slap and
_ stuff – sorted!

Part Three

Glit___
How not to ___
pants in clothes.

First published 2004 by
Walker Books Limited, 87 Vauxhall
Walk, London SE11 5HJ 10 9 8 7 6 5 4 3 2 1
Text © 2004 Jeanne Willis Illustrations © 2004
Lydia Monks The right of Jeanne Willis and Lydia
Monks to be identified as author and illustrator
respectively of this work has been asserted by them in
accordance with the Copyright, Designs and Patents Act
1988 This book has been typeset in Clichee and Tree
Printed in China All rights reserved British Library
Cataloguing in Publication data: a catalogue record for
this book is available from the British Library
ISBN 0-7445-8684-4

WALKER BOOKS

AND SUBSIDIARIES

LONDON · BOSTON · SYDNEY · AUCKLAND

www.walkerbooks.co.uk

Body Blitz

"Am I fit or what?"

How to look good, even on bad days!

Oi, Gorgeous! Yes, YOU!

Fed up with seeing images of "perfect" women?

Guess what, they don't exist! Top models have spotty bums. Pop divas have hairy legs. Even princesses have cellulite – hurrah! Nobody's perfect.

But there's loads you can do to make sure you look your beautiful best. Like eating the right stuff. Like getting off the couch. Like knowing what suits you. Why bother? Simple! If you look good, you feel good. And if you feel good, you'll be one happy bunny. Here's how...

Q I've got no boobs, stumpy legs and a bum like a football – who's gonna love me with a figure like mine?

Right now, there are hundreds of guys out there who are madly in love with small-bosomed, short girls like you. Having a bum like a football has to be an added bonus – two of their favourite things in one! Don't be fooled into thinking that you have to have legs and boobs like Barbie to be beautiful. You want proof? Next time you're at the shops, look at the women who are part of happy couples. Do they have figures like supermodels? No! They come in all shapes and sizes. You might not think they look beautiful, but their men do! And so will yours.

5

Q *I'm slim everywhere else, but my thighs are like tree trunks. Why?*

Women's shapes vary enormously but there are three basic body types: endomorphs, mesomorphs and ectomorphs. You inherit your body type, so if your mum had crusher thighs, so might you. If you're a mesomorph, it's no good trying to diet your luscious legs away. You may lose a bit of weight but it's more likely to come off somewhere else – like your boobs. If you really want to change your body shape, your best bet is to do exercises that target the area you want to firm up – see pages 14–15.

GET THIS!

The gluteus maximus in the buttock is the biggest muscle in a woman's body.

What's My Body Type?

ENDOMORPH: delicate bone structure, short legs, small feet, most likely to gain weight on tum.

MESOMORPH: the classic pear shape – hips larger than shoulders, legs the same length as torso, most likely to gain weight on thighs and bum.

ECTOMORPH: strong bone structure, long legs, does not gain weight easily – if they do, it doesn't all end up in one place.

Q Me and my mate look like twins and often wear identical clothes. We're the same size, so why do they always look better on her?

It could be to do with the way she carries herself. Look at the picture and see the huge effect good and bad posture can have on your appearance.

TAMMY AND TINA THE TWIN

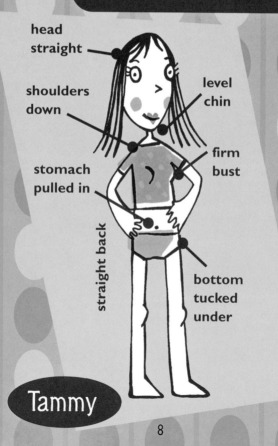

head straight

level chin

shoulders down

firm bust

stomach pulled in

straight back

bottom tucked under

Tammy

✪ Tammy weighs the same as Tina but looks slimmer because her stomach is pulled in.

✪ The twins are the same bra size, but Tina's bust looks droopy because she hunches over.

✪ Tammy is as shy as Tina, but she looks confident because she keeps her head up.

✪ Tammy is the same height as Tina, but she looks taller because her back is straight.

✪ The twins are the same hip size, but Tina's bum looks bigger because it isn't tucked in.

PERFORM THE POSTURE TEST

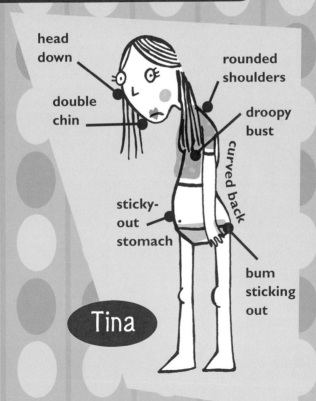

head down

rounded shoulders

double chin

droopy bust

curved back

sticky-out stomach

bum sticking out

Tina

Q Help! I like PE, but I hate having to get undressed in front of everybody. I'm sure they're all staring at me.

And everyone else is sure you're staring at them! There are all sorts of reasons why we feel embarrassed about our bodies – some girls think they're too fat or too thin, or less developed or more developed than their friends. Others feel shy because they have a skin problem or a scar. We rarely see each other naked, so no wonder we don't know what "normal" bodies are meant to look like. The truth is, although girls' bodies vary enormously, most of these variations are normal. Even so, feeling confident about showing your body is easier said than done. Hopefully, these changing-room tips will help...

Changing-Room Tips

✳ Remember to wear clean, flattering underwear on PE days – baggy or too-tight knickers won't do you any favours.

✳ If you don't wear a bra but you're embarrassed about your budding chest, wear a crop top.

✳ When you get undressed, pull your stomach in – you'll look much slimmer.

✳ If you have to shower, bring a big towel to school so you can cover up completely.

✳ Wear a skirt instead of trousers on PE days so you can pull shorts on underneath.

✳ If you have acne on your back or chest, avoid low-cut swimming costumes.

GET THIS!

The phrase "You can never be too thin or too rich" was coined by The Duchess of Windsor (who was too thin and too rich).

Q I hate sport, but people keep telling me to exercise. I'm not fat – why should I bother?

It's rotten having to do something you hate. Many grown women shudder at the memory of being forced to leap after a soggy netball in a freezing playground.

There's not a lot you can do to get out of school sports unless you throw a sickie, but your PE teacher won't fall for that old trick. Everyone needs to exercise to stay healthy, whether they're slim, fat, young or old. But if you're not the sporty type, there are plenty of ways to keep fit which don't involve balls, bats or PE mats. You don't even need to join a gym.

Try and do something active for at least 30 minutes a day. (That's only as long as one episode of your favourite soap!) You don't have to choose a "sport" – just do something to make your heart beat faster that doesn't make you collapse in a sweaty heap. One of the easiest ways to clock up your minimum 30 minutes a day is to walk whenever you can – you don't even have to do it all in one go. Walk to school, take the dog out, use stairs instead of lifts – or go mad and do all three! It'll become a habit you don't even think about.

GOOD THINGS ABOUT EXERCISE

☐ IT STOPS YOU FEELING LIKE A SAD, SOFA-DWELLING SLUG.

☐ IT GIVES YOU MORE BIRTHDAYS, BECAUSE IT PROTECTS YOU FROM DEADLY DISEASES.

☐ IT STOPS YOU BECOMING A SAGGY OLD BAG.

☐ IT MAKES YOUR SKIN GLOW (SAVES POUNDS ON MAKE-UP) AND GIVES YOU ENERGY TO PARTY!

☐ IT EVEN REDUCES THE MISERY OF PMT!

☐ UNFIT ISN'T A GOOD LOOK.

BLITZ THAT ANNOYING BODY PART!
Try doing these exercises
three times a week.
(Always remember to warm up first.)

EXER-THIGHSES

The Ballerina

1. Stand with your feet a metre apart. Turn your toes out as far as possible, pointing away from each other. (Heels should be turned in, pointing towards each other.)
2. Keep your shoulders back and your stomach and bum in. Put your hands on your hips.
3. Slowly start to sit, going down as far as you can. Hold for 2 seconds.
4. Slowly come back up and go right up onto your toes, lifting your arms above your head. (Remember to keep your shoulders down.)
5. Repeat 14 times.

Squats

1. Stand with your feet as wide as your shoulders, stomach pulled in, shoulders back.
2. Keeping your back straight, push your bottom out as though you're about to sit down. Go as far as you can and hold for a count of 3.
3. Push your bottom forward and scoop it upwards as you come up.
4. Repeat from the beginning, but this time with your arms stretched straight out in front as you go down. Pull them back as if you are rowing when you stand.
5. Repeat 14 times.

BLUBBERY BUTT BUSTERS

The Stork

1. Stand up straight and pull your stomach in. Without bending your back, stick one leg out straight behind you

with the toe pointed.
Take it up as far as you
can, keeping your leg
straight.
2. Repeat 10 times.
3. Change legs and
repeat.

Squeezy-bums

You can do this one
anywhere – even sitting
on a bus (unless it
makes you pull funny
faces).
1. Either sitting or
standing, clench your
buttocks together as
hard as you can.
2. Hold for a count of
three and release.
3. Repeat 10 times.

TERRIFIC TUMMY TONERS

Sit-ups

1. Lie on your back
with your knees up and
your feet apart, resting
on the floor.
2. Put your hands
behind your ears,
elbows out.
3. Pull your stomach in
and sit up as far as you
can. (Don't let your
chin drop onto your
chest – imagine there's
an apple under it.)
4. Hold the position for
a count of 2, then
lower yourself back
slowly.
5. Repeat 16 times.

The Plank

1. Lie on your stomach,
with your elbows on
the floor by your waist
and your hands
pressed together in
front of you.
2. Curl your toes
under and lift your
bum up so that your
knees are off the floor
and your back is
straight.
3. Supporting your
weight on your
forearms and toes,
suck your stomach in
as hard as you can and
hold it – imagine you
are trying to touch
your spine with your
belly button.
4. Keep holding it for
as long as you can,
pulling it in tighter
every few seconds ...
hold it ... hold it ... hold
it...
5. Relax for 30
seconds, then repeat
the exercise.

Q I've just bought a skirt to die for, but it's a little tight round the waist. What's the best way to lose a bit of weight?

1 EAT A BALANCED DIET. If you do this you'll get everything you need to stay fit and healthy. Try and eat 5 portions of fruit and vegetables every day. Some foods have more calories than others – e.g. bananas have more than raspberries – but don't get hung up on calories. A banana is better than a doughnut!

2 JACK IN THE JUNK. It's the easiest way to lose weight. You don't have to deny yourself chips and chocolate for ever – just go easy on foods high in fat and sugar. Start reading food labels – some "healthy foods", such as fruit yoghurts, cereals, muesli bars and even tinned peas, contain added sugar.

3 DON'T STARVE YOURSELF.
It's unhealthy and it doesn't work. OK, if you cut calories drastically you'll lose weight initially, but you'll put it all back on (plus a bit more, usually) when you start eating normally again. If your body suspects there's a food shortage, it hangs onto its fat reserves – if you try to diet again, you'll find it even harder to lose weight. It's called yo-yo dieting and it can actually make you fatter!

4 GET OFF YOUR BUTT.
Apart from the vitamins and minerals you need to stay healthy, food gives you energy. Every time you move, you burn up body fat. Walking burns about 300 calories an hour! The maths is simple:

sofa + junk food x 7 days = unfit, sad person
exercise + healthy food x 7 days = fit, happy person

Q My roommate at ballet school uses laxatives to help her lose weight – is it safe?

No, it's very dangerous. If you use laxatives (tablets that make you poo) too often it can cause dehydration, ruin your kidneys and stop your bowels working. What's more, it's useless as a slimming aid – in the time it takes for laxatives to work, the calories from food have already been absorbed by your body. Any weight you lose is just fluid, and even this is temporary because the body reacts by retaining water, so you feel bloated and can weigh up to 4.5 kg (10 pounds) more.

Some girls take diuretics (tablets that make you pee) to try and lose weight. These are equally dangerous and equally useless – the *only* way to lose weight permanently and safely is to eat a well-balanced diet and do enough exercise.

Q My friend always throws her packed lunch away. I'm sure she has an eating disorder – what should I do?

If someone has an eating disorder, they often do their utmost to hide it from their friends. Some girls say they've already eaten, or wear baggy clothes to disguise their weight loss. Others eat normally in public then vomit or use laxatives in secret. If your friend is obsessed with food and diets and gets angry or upset if you talk to her about it, she may have a problem and need help. If she won't talk to you, tell an adult that you are worried about her and why. She won't thank anyone for helping her right now, but she is in danger of ruining her health and needs expert advice.

Eating disorders

What	Why
ANOREXIA is when a person becomes obsessed with losing weight and deliberately starves themselves.	Often anorexia serves as a way of feeling in control – some girls stop eating becaus they're afraid of growing up. Others feel pressured into achieving an "ideal" figure.
BULIMIA is when someone binges on food then "gets rid of it" shortly afterwards by vomiting or taking laxatives and diuretics (purging).	People with bulimia are usually insecure – they often hate themselves but desperately want to please others. They are rarely overweight, but are convince they are fat.
BINGE-EATING DISORDER is when someone eats massive amounts in a very short time (less than 2 hours) until they feel uncomfortably full. If it happens twice a week for more than 6 months, it's a problem.	People who binge-eat are often obese and depressed. They go on diets, get hungry, then binge, or overeat, when they're unhappy or bored.
COMPULSIVE OVEREATING is when someone eats non-stop throughout the day and panics if no food is available.	Compulsive-eaters are addicted to food for emotion reasons instead of hunger. It often starts in childhood and happens to people who have never learnt to handle stressf situations. Some make themselves deliberately fat ar "unattractive" to avoid dealin with close relationships.

What to look out for & treatment

norexics may avoid eating situations, hide food or over-
xercise. They may wear baggy clothes to hide their weight
oss, and feel anxious or depressed or talk of suicide.
norexia has adverse effects on health and, in extreme
ases, can kill. Treatment may involve going into hospital to
tabilize weight. Therapy and medication can help others.

nging and purging are two symptoms to look out for –
nd these are usually done in secret. Food is comforting, so
hey binge and then feel ashamed of themselves. Purging
akes them feel "back in control". Like anorexia, bulimia
an kill, but it can be treated and the sooner someone gets
elp, the better.

hey may suffer from high blood pressure and are at risk
rom diabetes, heart disease and other serious illnesses.
inge-eating can be treated, but putting a binge-eater on a
et may make things worse. Some of the treatments used
r bulimia work for binge-eaters too, such as cognitive-
ehavioural therapy. This is where people are taught to
nderstand why they act the way they do and how to stop
hemselves doing it. Often a combination of therapies helps.

hey often suffer from severe weight gain and health
roblems associated with being overweight. Not all
verweight people are compulsive-eaters: compulsive-eaters
now their eating pattern is out of control. They may start
o lose self-pride, forget to wash or dress properly and feel
orthless and lethargic. Compulsive overeating can be
ured, and the best treatment includes therapy and
utritional counselling.

POO-O-E-E!

Q Help! I wash my feet every day, but when I take my trainers off, my feet are minging.

Feet have lots of sweat glands, and when you reach puberty, they can really go into overdrive – especially if they're trapped in trainers all day. If you want toes that smell like a rose, here goes...

HOW TO KEEP YOUR FEET SWEET

1 Wash feet every day and dry carefully between your toes.

2 After washing, use a foot deodorant (powder or spray), or ordinary talc in an emergency.

3 Wear clean socks or tights every day.

4 Avoid nylon socks. Natural fibres like cotton and wool are best – they let your skin breathe, so you get less sweaty.

5 Use special, deodorizing trainer-liners.

6 Don't wear the same pair of shoes two days running.

7 Go barefoot whenever possible.

8 Check for athlete's foot (a fungal infection) or verrucas (foot warts). If you suspect anything, describe it to the chemist or doctor and he'll give you some stuff to treat it.

GET THIS!
6% of girls are born with webbed feet.

9 Use small nail scissors to trim your toenails and cut them straight across so you don't get ingrowing toenails. File any edges but don't file down at the sides.

10 Gently push back your cuticles (the skin growing over the half-moon bit) with your thumbnail after you've had a bath.

Q When should I start using a deodorant?

POOH!

When no one will sit next to you on the bus! Seriously, you should consider wearing an underarm deodorant as soon as you suspect you're sweating more, which is usually around puberty. Fresh sweat doesn't whiff, but sweat trapped inside several layers of clothes rapidly causes BO (body odour). Synthetic fabrics like nylon make the problem worse. If you're not sure whether you need a deodorant (it's not always easy to detect your own smell) ask your mum or your best mate, or if that's too awful, sniff the armpit of your blouse a few hours after you've taken it off. If it smells like an old tomcat, buy an antiperspirant deodorant and get into the habit of using it every day ... please?!

How to avoid BO
– it's the pits!

⭐ Wash under your arms every day.

⭐ Ordinary body sprays don't stop BO. Use an antiperspirant deodorant – this will minimize the amount of sweat you produce and keep you sweet.

⭐ Remember to reapply deodorant after you've been swimming or had a shower.

⭐ You can buy handy deodorant wipes to keep in your bag for emergencies.

⭐ If you prefer, health shops sell antiperspirant "stones", which keep you fresh without any chemicals.

⭐ Roll-on, gel or stick deodorants last longer than sprays.

Worst Case Scenario

HELP! I'm going to a disco in like 5 minutes but my mum forgot to wash my one and only favourite top and the armpits stink!

1 If you have a tumble-dryer, bung in the offending top with a sheet of fabric softener. Or use a dry-cleaning sheet and put it with the top in the bag provided. Let it whizz around for as long as poss – it should take the edge off. (Use the cool cycle if the label says dry-clean only.)

2 Spray the armpits lightly with a fabric freshener, or at a pinch, use one of those ironing sprays and iron it. (Check the label says it's OK to iron your top!)

3 Turn the top inside out and spray the armpits lightly with an aerosol deodorant – it's a last resort, but hey, you're desperate.

4 Never try and cover it up with half a gallon of perfume. You'll end up smelling of too much perfume – and BO!

Q My best friend said I had bad breath. Help!

Don't worry! Everyone – including your best friend – gets halitosis (bad breath) from time to time. It can be easily prevented.

BAD BREATH: THE MAIN CAUSES

poor mouth hygiene/gum disease

drinking alcohol

eating strong foods

not eating properly

hormonal imbalance

dry mouth

smoking

upset stomach

BAD BREATH: HOW TO CURE IT

★ Go for regular dental check-ups.
★ If the dentist gives you the all-clear, try brushing up on your tooth-cleaning regime.
★ If you need to freshen breath when you're out and about, chew sugar-free gum or carry special breath-fresheners – these come in tablets or sprays.
★ If your bad breath still persists, see a doctor to rule out any stomach disorders.

Q There's a gang of girls at school and they all smoke. They said if I had a cigarette I could hang out with them – there can't be any harm in having one fag, can there?

It isn't one fag that does the damage, it's getting addicted to them. Wanting to be part of the in-crowd can be really hard to resist, but what if you can't stop smoking? Fag Ash Lil is *not* a great look when you're older (and you *will* get older!). Older smokers don't look glam, they just look desperate – check them out at the bus stop if you don't believe it. Smoker's cough and smelly breath isn't sexy either. Telling you not to smoke will only make you more determined to have a puff, so look at the facts, then decide – it's your life.

SMOKING – THE FACTS

☞ It's against the law to smoke until you're 16.

☞ The nicotine in cigarettes is highly addictive. 99% of teenagers who smoke started by "just having the odd fag".

☞ Cigarette smoking is the major cause of preventable death in this country. Nearly all lung cancer patients are smokers. Smokers are twice as likely to suffer from heart disease and peptic ulcers. Smokers run a far greater risk of developing throat, mouth, oesophageal, pancreatic, kidney, bladder and cervical cancer.

☞ Tobacco stains your teeth, fingers and hair yellow and gives you bad breath.

☞ Smoking turns your skin grey and ages it prematurely, especially the upper lip, which becomes permanently puckered.

☞ Smoking at a young age can scar your lungs, which makes you more likely to get lung disease later in life – even if you quit.

☞ Nicotine poisoning can cause nausea, dizziness and weakness – which is why you feel like puking up when you first smoke.

☞ Smoking is expensive – loads of your spending money will go up in smoke.

☞ Smoking harms the people around you.

Oooh, look - **carrots!**

Q Help! Every time we go to a party, my mate drinks too much and throws up – I'm really worried about her.

Most teenagers overdo it once in a while, but you're right to worry. Overdosing on alcohol can be deadly. Around 6,000 15–20-year-olds die every year from alcohol-related causes. If someone who has been drinking passes out or has trouble breathing, get medical help fast – an unconscious person can choke to death on their vomit. It is against the law to buy alcohol if you're under 18, but if you are going to drink alcohol, learn to do it safely.

ALL ABOUT ALCOHOL

🍷 The more alcohol a drink contains, the stronger it is. Beer contains around 5%. Wine 9–12%. Spirits 40% or more. Don't mix your drinks – it'll make you feel sick or give you a hangover.

🍷 Don't drink on an empty stomach – it'll go straight to your head.

🍷 Girls get drunk quicker than blokes after drinking the same amount. We produce less of the enzyme that breaks down alcohol – so don't try and drink your man under the table.

🍷 Alcohol dulls your reflexes – that's why you should never get into a car if the driver has been drinking, even if they don't seem or look drunk.

🍷 Never walk home on your own if you've had a skinful (drunk girls are vulnerable to muggers/rapists/road accidents). If no one can take you home, call a cab. Any parent would rather pay at the other end than have you dead in a ditch – you'll be grounded, but hey, you'll be alive!

🍷 Alcohol relaxes you, but too much can make the coolest person behave like a prat. At best, you'll embarrass yourself. At worst, you'll do something really dumb, like having sex without using contraception.

🍷 Pace yourself – if you knock drinks back too quickly, you'll get drunk. Alcohol makes you pee a lot, so it dehydrates you. Drink plenty of water in between drinks and some more before you go to bed to avoid getting a hangover.

🍷 If you do drink too much, you may feel dizzy, clammy and sick, and will possibly vomit. Ask a friend to look after you and help you get home.

Q Why should I say "no" to drugs? My mate gets a buzz out of them and feels fine.

Drugs and their effects

What	Effects
CANNABIS (marijuana, pot, weed, hash, grass, spliff, ganga): Flowers, leaves or resin are smoked in a cigarette (joint), in a water pipe (bong) or eaten in cakes.	Various – from feeling happy and laid-back to tiredness, headach paranoia and hung (the munchies).
INHALANTS: Solvents in paint-thinner, glue, lighter fluid, gas, etc. are sprayed into a bag and sniffed.	Instant buzz, then drowsiness/ sedation. Hallucinations, headache and nausea.
TRANQUILLIZERS (benzodiazepines) (Valium, Rohypnol, etc.): Prescription drugs in the form of tablets, capsules, injections or suppositories.	Calming, relief fron tension and anxiety High doses can make you drowsy and forgetful.

Let's be honest. Certain drugs can make
you feel good, otherwise no one would take
them. But what's also true is that the same
drug that makes your mates feel great
could make you feel ill, frightened or worse.
It's impossible to tell what's in the drug or
how strong it is. Even if you only try it
once, you're taking a risk – you could
overdose or even die. No drugs are 100%
safe, and most are illegal.
Check the facts...

Risks and addiction rate

Long-term effects are not known, but it can cause
memory loss, slowed reflexes, personality changes and
may affect your fertility. May cause serious harm to an
unborn child.
Low addiction rate.

One-time use and overdose can lead to instant death
through cardiac arrest/lack of oxygen. Suffocation/choking
on vomit. Accidents due to feeling "drunk"/serious burns
(many solvents are flammable).
High addiction rate.

Dangerous if mixed with alcohol. Some tranquillizers
cause temporary loss of short-term memory. Risk of
panic attacks when trying to quit. Injecting crushed
tablets or contents of capsules is very dangerous.
High addiction rate.

What	Effects
COCAINE (coke, blow, crack, snow, C): A white powder snorted or injected or smoked. (Crack is a smokable, chemically-altered cocaine.)	Sense of wellbein energy, anxiety, p reduced appetite The "high" is followed by a cra
AMPHETAMINE AND METHAMPHETAMINE (speed, meth, crank, crystal, ice, dexies, hearts, whizz, black beauties): Found in diet pills, prescription medicines. Snorted, smoked, swallowed or injected.	Increased energy alertness, short-l euphoria.
ECSTASY (MDMA) (X, XTC, E): Pills made in illegal labs.	Energy and alertness, happin loving feelings.
LSD (lysergic acid diethylamide) (acid, trip): A hallucinogenic (distorts sense of time, vision, sound, etc.). Absorbed on paper (blotter) or a sugar cube and chewed. Also tablets/capsules.	Hallucinations, seeing bright colours, out-of-b experiences, ecst feeling, sweating, palpitations, naus
MAGIC MUSHROOMS: Specific type of mushroom, dried and then eaten whole or mixed in food/drink.	Same as LSD.
HEROIN (smack, mojo, horse, junk, skag): In pure form, a white powder (dried "milk" of opium poppy). Can be smoked or snorted but a more intense high comes from injecting it straight into veins.	Pleasure rush an low sensitivity to pain. Depresses nervous system, causing heart an breathing proble

Risks and addiction rate

asy to overdose, leads to seizures, heart attack, stroke.
epeated use causes paranoia, insomnia and hallucinations.
isk of AIDS and hepatitis from shared needles if injected.
igh addiction rate.

igh risk of overdose, convulsions, coma, death from heart
ailure, ruptured vessels in brain. Can be fatal if combined
ith exercise, due to increased body temperature. Risk of
IDS and hepatitis from shared needles if injected. Long-
erm use: hallucinations, violence, paranoia.
igh addiction rate.

erious risk of overdose, heart attack, increased body
emperature (causing lethal dehydration), seizures and
eath, especially when combined with physical activity
dancing, etc.). Long-term use: teeth-clenching, shakes, dry
outh, nausea and cramps, possibly liver and brain damage.
ddiction rate unknown.

Bad trips", convulsions, coma, heart and lung failure, high
sk of accidents. Often laced with rat poison, causing brain
amage or death. Long-term use: scary visual memories
lashbacks) replayed any time later.
**ddiction rate: often causes psychological
ependency.**

ausea, increased blood pressure, bad trips, mistaking
oisonous mushrooms for magic ones.
ow addiction rate.

igh risk of death by overdose, even on first try. Risk of
IDS or hepatitis from shared needles if injected. Runny
ose and stomach cramp. Heroin may be laced with
uinine/other dangerous substances.
**igh addiction rate. Withdrawal (cold turkey) is
wful.**

STUFF YOU NEED TO KNOW ABOUT THE DRUGS SCENE

✪ All drugs carry risks – even an overdose of vitamin pills can kill.

✪ Some drugs can kill the first time you use them.

✪ Many drugs are "cut" or mixed with other stuff. There's no way of telling what's in them – could be talc, toilet cleaner or rat poison.

Oh, go on, try it!
It's wicked!

✪ Drugs have different effects on different people. A friend may take the same stuff and be OK – you might end up in hospital, or worse.

✪ Drugs are even more risky if you're taking other medication – it can cause a dangerous chemical reaction.

✪ Drugs and alcohol can be a really deadly combo.

✪ Sharing needles is a great way to catch hepatitis and AIDS. Hepatitis can be fatal. There is no cure for AIDS.

✪ Drugs are expensive – if you become addicted, you will have to fund your habit. Unless you're rich, you may have to steal to pay for them.

✪ Drug dealers are criminals – if you become addicted, you'll have to face some seriously scary people who don't give a toss whether you live or die. They may force you to "work" for them if you owe them money – probably as a prostitute.

✪ Coming off addictive drugs can be truly awful.

GET THIS!

The cannabis plant used to be harvested for fibre to make clothes and rope.

The end of the chapter – the start of a NEW YOU?

Are you raring to be toned, honed and glowing with health? What's that? You would take more exercise – only there's something good on telly? You would eat more fruit – but it seems a shame to let this pizza go to waste? OK, so you're only human. There's a time and a place for fast food and chilling out, but not every night of the week, eh? If you want to look your beautiful best (and you know you do), it ain't gonna happen if you're a total slob.

So why not make yourself a little promise? "From now on, I will do at least one healthy thing every day." It could be a big thing, like saying no to fags. Or a little thing, like cutting back on burgers and walking to places instead of calling DadCabs. The more you do, the fitter you'll feel. The fitter you feel, the more fantastic you'll look ... and it won't just be you who notices! Go for it!

You only get one body.

Give it some loving.

Part Two

Zits

"Anyone got a paper bag?"

How to make
the most of your skin,
make-up and hair

Natural beauty...

is a wonderful thing. Some of us are lucky enough to have it, but there are days when nature could do with a helping hand. Or a good slap. Maybe we want to disguise a spot or get rid of a shiny nose. Or maybe we just love playing with glitter and different looks. In either case, it really does help to know your lipstick from your lip wax.

However, true beauty doesn't lie in the bottom of a make-up bag. Lots of girls don't want to wear make-up, so never feel you have to. Fresh skin and healthy hair are really all you need. If your face is a juvenile disgrace and every day is a bad hair day, don't put a paper bag over it! Read on. You SHALL go to the ball!

Q Help! My face looks like a pizza - why am I so spotty?

Lots of people get spots in their teens. When your hormone levels change, your

skin can produce too much sebum (the oily
stuff which keeps it soft and waterproof).
If that happens, your face looks shiny and
your hair follicles may become blocked.
If you're lucky, you'll get the odd spot on
the end of your nose (always before a
party!) and a few blackheads. If you're
unlucky, you can end up looking like a
target practice with red pustules and fluid-
filled cysts – in other words, acne. Spots
often get worse just before your period or
if you are stressed. They can be painful
and embarrassing, but there are things you
can do to make them a whole lot better ...
read on!

Zit Myths

Acne is contagious – FALSE! You can't catch acne off a spotty guy.

Greasy food gives you spots – FALSE! Chips and chocolate might make you fat, but spots are caused by hormones.

You get spots because you don't wash enough – FALSE! Dirt doesn't cause spots – excess sebum does.

You can't inherit acne – FALSE! (Sadly, you can...)

You will grow out of your spots – er ... FALSE! Most people do, but some poor creatures have acne right into their 40s and beyond.

You only get acne on your face – FALSE! You can get it on your neck, back, chest, thighs and – shock horror – on your bum!

HOW TO ZAP ZITS

☐ Don't over-wash or over-cleanse your skin – it makes it even oilier.

☐ Avoid harsh "de-greasing", abrasive or perfumed cleansers and soaps. Find a mild cleanser to suit your skin.

☐ If your skin needs a deep cleanse, use a mud pack (this might make your skin break out, so don't use it the day before a party).

☐ Use a light moisturizer – even oily skin needs moisturizing.

☐ There are lots of different spot creams you can try – don't use too much, though, as they can be very drying.

☐ If things get really bad, go and see your doctor. There are several things you could try that may work, including antibiotics and powerful zit-zapping drugs. You'll need to discuss what is suitable for you.

BIG PUS-FILLED ZIT WITH HEAD

Oh, go on then, but don't make a habit of it. You're not supposed to squeeze spots, as it can spread infection and cause scars if you're not careful. Try and do it the night before if you must, or the spot will "weep" and be difficult to cover up. Here's how:

1 Wash hands and make sure your nails are short or you'll break your skin.

2 Hold a hot wet flannel on the spot for 30 seconds to soften it up.

3 Using a sterile needle, carefully "prick" the head of the spot – just nick the top.

4 Wrap tissues around your fingers and *gently* push the spot from either side until all the pus comes out ... splat! Make sure it's all out or it'll build up again.

5 Dab the spot with antiseptic lotion.

6 If the spot bleeds, put a little piece of tissue on it until it stops, then let the air get to it for as long as possible before using concealer/powder.

BIG RED "BLIND" SPOT

Never squeeze these – they will just get angrier. Cover them! Here's how:

1 Clean the spot and smooth away any crusty bits round the edge.

2 Dab a spot cover stick onto the spot quite heavily in the centre, then tap it into the surrounding skin until it's blended. Don't use liquid foundation – it will slide off and the spot will show by lunchtime.

3 Pat all over your face with all-in-one or powder foundation – be generous!

4 You now look like an explosion in a flour factory, so, using your fat complexion brush, whisk off excess powder for a natural, long-lasting finish.

Q Help! There are so many different types of foundation, I don't know which to use.

If you have normal skin with no spots, you probably don't need foundation – you lucky thing! If you haven't got a perfect complexion, foundation can add colour, even out skin tone, minimize blemishes and work as a base for the rest of your make-up. Find one that suits your skin type and colour. Choose matt for oily skin or moisturized for dry skin.

HOW TO RECOGNIZE YOUR SKIN TYPE

1. Smooth skin, closed pores, matt complexion, occasional spot = NORMAL

2. Rough patches, flaky skin, feels tight after washing, no spots = DRY

3. Shiny "T-zone" with open pores, smooth cheeks = COMBINATION

4. Shine appears soon after cleansing, blackheads, prone to spots = OILY

TYPES OF FOUNDATION:

MOUSSE:
This is light and glides on easily – but it also glides off if you have oily skin. Good for dry or normal skins.

TINTED:

Great for young, dry and blemish-free normal skins – this doesn't do a cover-up job, it just adds a natural glow to your skin. Avoid if you have oily skin, or, like Rudolph, you'll have a very shiny nose.

STICK/ PANCAKE:

Great coverage – best applied with a damp sponge. But unless you're on stage, it can look too heavy on young skins.

LIQUID:

This gives light to medium coverage. Good for evening out skin tone but avoid on oily skins. Rubbish at covering spots, as it can slide off or get caked on the crusty bits.

POWDER:

Perfect for girls with normal, oily or combo skins who can't get to grips with foundation. Just press onto your skin with a puff for good coverage and a natural matt finish. Brush off any excess with a complexion brush.

ALL ~IN~ONE:

This comes in solid cream or powder form in a compact with its own sponge. Easy to apply, not too heavy and gives good coverage on all skin types. Used over a spot cover, it is ideal for blemished skin.

Q How do I know which is the right colour foundation?

Always ask for a few testers first. Dab them on your jawline and check them in the daylight. The right colour will disappear into your skin.

Q I look like I've been sunbathing under a sieve. How can I get rid of my freckles?

Freckles are small, flat spots of skin pigment – there is nothing you can do to get rid of them. To stop them getting worse, use a sunblock (it'll stop you getting a tan, though). You can disguise freckles with spot concealer or minimize them with foundation. Just bear in mind that lots of us find freckles really cute – some girls buy special pencils to draw fake ones on!

101, 102, 103, 104...

How to remove make-up

Always remove your make-up before you go to bed or you'll end up with dull skin, puffy eyes and filthy pillows.

BLIMEY –
what a
night!

1 Remove eye make-up first. If you can't afford a flashy eye make-up remover, good old baby oil works well, even on waterproof mascara. Pour a little onto cotton wool, close eyes and remove with downward strokes, taking care not to drag delicate skin round the eye.

2 Use a mild cleanser to remove foundation and lipstick.

3 Rinse face and pat dry with a clean towel, or use a mild toner to remove any last traces of make-up.

4 Moisturize dry and normal areas, and around eyes. Apply spot treatment to zits.

TOP LIPSTICK TRICKS

Lipstick can light up your face and make you look wonderful – or it can go horribly wrong and make you look like you've had a fight with some jammy toast. To avoid a full-blown lippy disaster, read on...

✪ Vivid, dark or bright lipsticks look too "dolly" on young faces – like a kid who's raided her mum's make-up bag! Go for natural glossy or pearly shades.

✪ Light-coloured lipstick makes your mouth look bigger. Dark lipstick makes thin lips look like slits.

✪ Choosing a shade to suit your clothes or nail varnish often works – that doesn't mean black lipstick with a black dress!

✪ Don't put lippy on cracked lips – eeugh!

✪ To give lipstick more staying power, blot lips with foundation first. Don't go over the edges to make your mouth look bigger – Coco the Clown is not a good look.

✪ Blot excess lippy with a tissue.

✪ Vaseline makes good, cheap lip gloss.

✪ Check for lipstick on your teeth.

✪ Smile! It'll do much more for your looks.

HOW TO CUSTOMIZE YOUR EYES

Eyes are the windows to your soul, or so they say. If it's true, make the most of your windows with these tips.

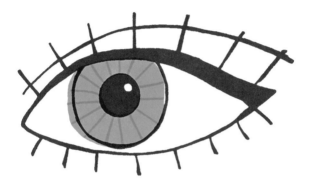

1 Powder eyeshadows stay on better than cream ones.

2 Wear natural colours in the day – it looks right and it's less obvious when they wear off or crease. Dark ones can look really manky by lunchtime.

3 Eye pencils are easier to use than liquid eyeliner. Choose one with a soft texture.

4 Dark eyelashes make eyes look bigger. If yours are pale but you don't like mascara, dye them. You can buy kits or go to a salon. It lasts up to six weeks.

5 If your eyelashes are straight, eyelash-curlers give a wide-awake effect.

Q I'd love to wear nail polish but I always make a mess of it – what's the secret?

You need a steady hand and time for it to dry. You can't rush a nail job, so don't leave it until the last minute, or you'll smudge it. If you're not used to painting your nails, stick to pale, pearly colours – the mistakes don't show as much and they don't look as grotty as dark shades if they chip.

TOP TIPS FOR POLISHED TALONS

✳ Don't use old nail polish – it goes gunky in the bottle really quickly. Get yourself a new bottle of base coat (to stop your nails staining), a coloured polish (to match clothes or lipstick) and a top coat (to prevent chipping).

✳ Give yourself a manicure first – remove old polish, push back any cuticles and file your nails.

✳ Wash and dry hands.

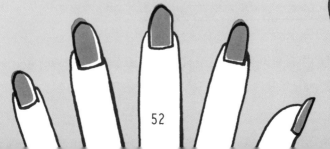

✳ Roll bottle between your palms to mix varnish properly.

✳ Load brush with base coat (but not so it's dripping). The idea is to put a *thin* coat of polish on, not a fat blobby one. Keep your hand steady and quickly stroke the brush from the base to the tip, starting in the middle. Three strokes should do it – one in the middle, two on each side. Don't go over the bit you've just done – it'll pucker.

✳ Paint each nail and wait until dry.

✳ Apply a coat of coloured polish using the three-stroke method and let it dry. You may need a second coat, in which case brush it on and let it dry.

✳ Finish with a top coat, then wait ... wait ... wait ... don't touch anything! Don't stroke the cat or pull your tights up for about an hour. When you think it's dry, dab a finger gently onto your thumbnail to check – if it's tacky, wait some more!

✳ When it's absolutely dry, slap on some hand cream and off you go!

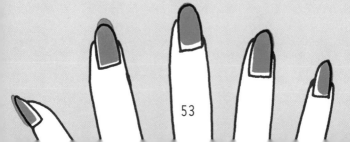

Q Help! I need a new haircut, but I'm scared it'll go wrong.

A great haircut can make you feel like a new woman – but what if it's the *wrong* woman?! Here's how to avoid a cut-astrophe...

No, REALLY, it's all the rage!

1 Get to know your hair... Is it curly, frizzy, straight, spiky or wavy? Is it greasy, dry or normal? Is it thick, fine, limp, flyaway or coarse? What do you dislike about it? Too long? Too short? Too difficult to manage? Too young? Too old-fashioned?

2 Find a new look... Tie your hair back and look at the shape of your face in a mirror. Is it round, square, heart-shaped, long, thin or oval? Find a pile of magazines and pull out pictures of models with similar face shapes to yours. Cut out and keep the ones with haircuts that you like.

3 Think about whether the haircut you're after suits your lifestyle. Is it worth spending hours blow-drying a "do" that's going to spend its time in a swimming pool?

4 Can you afford to go to the hairdresser's every six weeks? Short, precise cuts need regular trims to keep them in shape.

5 Find a brilliant hairdresser – if one of your mates has a great haircut, find out where she had it done and make an appointment for a consultation. It's usually free and it's your chance to discuss the kind of look you want with the stylist. Take your magazine pictures with you but don't set your heart on having an identical cut.

6 If you liked the stylist, if her suggestions were good ones and if you felt she listened to you, book in!

7 Take someone you trust to keep you company and give you support.

Q How do I get rid of dandruff?

Dandruff isn't catching, but snowy shoulders aren't cool. Flaky bits can be caused by not rinsing properly, a build-up of styling products or a dry scalp. Real dandruff is caused by a microbe which speeds up skin-shedding. It can happen if you're run-down, have an allergy or if your hormones are going loco. Ask your chemist for a treatment shampoo – it should knock your dandruff on the head in about 3 weeks. If it doesn't, see your doctor – you may have eczema or psoriasis, which she can treat in other ways.

Q I hate my curls! How can I get rid of them?

Why are none of us happy with what we've been given? It's nature's way of letting us play hairdressers, of course! If you want straight, sleek hair, there are loads of electric hair-straighteners around that do a great temporary job. Permanent hair-straightening involves chemicals that break

GET THIS!

Hair grows between 5 and 15 mm a week!

down the structure of your hair. It lasts for ages but can make your hair brittle.

Q I hate having straight hair – how can I make it curly?

Try some of these temporary tricks to see if Curls R U, and if you love the look, you could go for something more permanent – like a perm!

HOW TO CURL UP FOR THE NIGHT

Benders

Rollers/ heated rollers

Perming

Spray

Curling tongs

HAVING A BAD HAIR DAY?

The only people who don't have bad hair days are bald. Hair that won't do as it's told can be caused by all sorts of things:

- ✪ Static electricity in the air
- ✪ Lying in a strange position
- ✪ Someone putting a curse on you
- ✪ Change in diet
- ✪ Illness
- ✪ Hormones
- ✪ Using different shampoo/conditioner
- ✪ The weather
- ✪ Washing in different water (e.g. if you go on holiday, the water may be harder/softer)
- ✪ Nylon pillowcases

It must have been my pillowcase...

GET A GRIP

Laugh in the face of
bad hair days by
getting a grip,
some slides and
some hair bands, etc.
Pin, plait, twist, bead or
braid your hair into place.
Show it who's boss – and
if all else fails, get a hat!

WHICH HAIRBRUSH?

TYPE	PROS & CONS
Small, round brush	Good for making tight curls.
Semi-circular brush	Good for creating bounce rather than waves when blow-drying.
Natural bristle brush	Grips hair well for styling but can break it – be gentle.
Synthetic bristle brush	Hairdressers prefer this type – gentle on wet hair and easy to clean. Can slip slightly when styling.
Round-tipped brush	Good for brushing wet hair and for sore scalps, as it doesn't scratch.

GET THIS!
You lose about 80 hairs a day.

If you can get to a chemist, buy one of those puff-in, brush-out shampoos – it'll absorb the oil and make your hair look and smell fresh in an instant.

If you can't get hold of any dry shampoo, use talcum powder. Don't shake it too hard or you'll end up looking like a spook – just sprinkle a little bit onto your scalp, massage it in gently, leave for a few minutes, then brush it out.

If you've got dark hair, dry shampoo can make you look a bit dusty, so try this:

1. Add a teaspoon of strained lemon or lime juice to half a cup of warm water.

2. Use a cotton-wool ball and dab the mixture over your scalp to absorb the grease – it'll bring back the shine, too.

Q I want to get my ears pierced – will it hurt?

Not much and only for a second – it just feels like a hard pinch. Don't let your mate do it with the compasses out of your maths set – go to a reputable salon or big department store.

Err, shouldn't you wash them...?

Most use an ear-piercing gun – a stapling device which "shoots" a stud earring through your lobe. You need to keep the earring in or the hole will close up. Twist it regularly and keep it clean with surgical spirit. Oh, and don't wear hoops for PE – if they get caught, you'll rip your ear lobe.

Q I want to get a tattoo but my mum says I've got to wait until I'm 16 – why is she being so boring?

Most reputable tattoo parlours won't take you on unless you're over 16. You can lie about your age, but before you take the plunge, think carefully about the following – for your *own* sake.

❤ It's permanent! It might fade a little, but it will never wash off. It can sometimes be removed with lasers, but don't bank on it. Why not try a non-permanent tattoo first?

❤ It hurts! To create a design, insoluble dye is injected beneath your skin with a needle. Having a design on your lower back is particularly painful.

❤ A cute little fish on your tummy will turn into a big fat whale if you get pregnant – and it'll turn into a wrinkly whale when you're an old lady.

❤ When you get older, other people might judge you by your tattoo.

❤ Whatever you do, make sure you go to a reputable parlour and that they use a new, sterile needle on you – a contaminated needle could give you hepatitis or AIDS.

Part Three

Glitz

"Does my bum look big in this?"

We get to the bottom of your style problems

Q What should I wear to make me look taller and slimmer?

Stilts and a tent? No really, there are lots of tried-and-tested tricks that can make you look taller and a whole dress-size smaller...

WEAR DARK COLOURS: Black, grey, dark green, navy, brown and deep purple make you look instantly slimmer. White trousers will never, ever disguise a lardy bum. And pale pink or fawn just make you look naked.

WEAR ONE COLOUR ALL OVER: Mixing colours can chop you in half and make you look chunky.

64

WEAR BIG, IRREGULAR PATTERNS: These make large areas look smaller.

WEAR THIN, VERTICAL STRIPES: These make you look extra-willowy. Avoid horizontal stripes – they would even make a stick insect look chubby.

WEAR SLIGHTLY FITTED STUFF: If you're short and large, you'll look a million times lovelier in clothes with a bit of shape to them. Don't wear clingy stuff – it just screams, "Hey, here's my fat bit!" Instead, buy clothes that skim *over* your squishy bits.

WEAR MATT FABRICS: Shiny, floaty, glittery fabric shouts, "Whey-hey! Look at this!" Only use it to draw attention to your best features – fab shoulders, great bosoms, a tiny waist, etc.

WEAR THE RIGHT SKIRT LENGTH: If you've got mini-legs, maxi-skirts will drown you. Go for something that ends around the knee or higher if you've got slim pins.

WEAR WELL-FITTING TROUSERS: For max skinniness and height, wear well-fitting (never skin-tight) trousers that skim your body. Check they're not too tight around the waist or you'll squish over the sides!

Q My boobs look really small, even in a padded bra – how can I make them look bigger?

Try wearing clingy tops, horizontal stripes, light colours and shiny fabric – these draw attention to what you've got. Avoid low-cut tops – high necklines make your bosoms look bigger. Make your waist look as small as possible by wearing wide, stretchy belts. This gives the illusion that you've got more up top than you really have. Dresses with darts will take the material in under your bust and make the most of your curves.

I can't
BREATHE!!!

Q I've got massive bosoms – how can I make them look smaller?

Oh, be quiet! You look fantastic and you know it. Sorry – just jealous! If you don't want to look like a Big Girl's Blouse, stick to dark colours. Avoid clingy, lycra tops and skimpy woollies – you'll look like you've shoplifted melons. Don't wear really low or high necklines – a modest V-neck will minimize your bust. Avoid shiny fabric, frills, ruffles and jewellery that draws attention to your cleavage. Wear single-breasted jackets – double-breasted ones will make you look as if you've got one huge boob.

Q My arms are so long that my handbag drags on the pavement. How can I make them look shorter?

Join a group of orang-utans? Failing that, you can disguise long arms by wearing three-quarter length sleeves or by pushing your long sleeves up to just below the elbow. Simple, but it works.

Q I look like a beanpole – I've got no curves. Help!

If you stand still long enough, you'll probably get booked by Models One. It's fashionable to look like you – tough on the rest of us, but if that's no comfort and you want more curves, here's what to do.

⭐ Wear a padded bra.

⭐ Wear light, bright colours – hot pinks, metallics and mad patterns.

⭐ Wear woolly, patterned tights – stripy ones add loads of curves.

⭐ Wear chunky knits, layers, textured material, fake fur, anything fluffy or ruffled.

⭐ Avoid wearing one dark colour all over – you'll look lanky.

⭐ Anything flared will make you look curvier, so flared jeans and flared skirts are good – long pencil skirts make you look like ... a long pencil.

Q Help! The gusset of my tights always ends up round my knees.

Wrong size, baby! Tights are usually sold in small, medium and large, but unfortunately, different brands measure up differently. Here are some tight dilemmas and solutions.

The half mast
The legs are too short. Try another brand that gives a height guide.

The stranglehold
The legs fit, but the waist's too tight. In an emergency, cut a little v-shape in the elastic at the sides – don't cut as far as the actual tights or they'll run. In future, try tights with a "comfort waistband".

The twist
Feels like one leg is on backwards? Take them off and start again. Make sure they are round the right way and ease them up slowly.

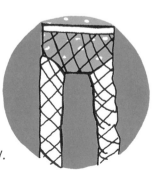

Q Help – my tights have got a ladder and I haven't got a spare pair.

Don't panic. You can stop the ladder getting worse by rubbing it with soap or painting it with clear nail varnish. If the ladder is in a really visible place, like on the top of your foot, wear your tights backwards.

HOW NOT TO LOOK PANTS IN KNICKERS

No matter how fab the outfit, the wrong pants make you look daft. Here are some classic Pants Faux Pas.

VPL (Visible Panty Line)
CAUSE: Pants too tight in the leg/the wrong shape for tight trousers or skirts.
CURE: Wear short-shaped briefs or a thong.

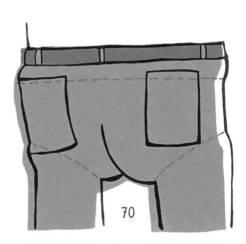

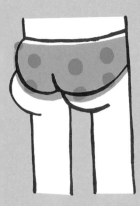

Two-faced Cheek
(pants up crack, creating four buttocks)
CAUSE: Pants badly cut or wrong shape for your bum.
CURE: Try a style that won't cut your buttocks in half – a thong, trouser-pants or briefs with lower-cut legs.

Seamy Sides (seams showing through tight clothing)
CAUSE: Frilly or seamed knickers showing through clothes.
CURE: Smooth, seamless knickers.

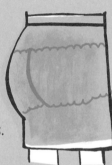

Dark Side of the Moon
CAUSE: Dark-coloured knickers under a light skirt.
CURE: Wear flesh-coloured knickers – or a slip (if you're over 50!).

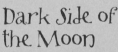

WARNING
Never go knickerless in tights unless they have a cotton-lined gusset – your pubes will go static and you'll get pimples on your bum!

Q Help! I've got a wardrobe full of clothes but nothing looks right.

Everybody suffers from wardrophobia now and then – that awful moment when you realize the fake fur trousers that looked so cool in the changing-room actually make you look like a pantomime horse. As you look in the mirror, you realize why those Lurex leggings were half price – no one else would be seen dead in them! Tired of being a fashion victim? The best way forward is to study

72

these common mistakes and avoid them like the plague.

1 Never shop with a tart, or a slob, or anyone else whose idea of fashion is wildly different from yours. They will try and get you to dress how they dress, and you may not look so good in rubber or pie-crust collars.

2 Don't buy the latest fashion if it doesn't suit you. Obvious, but it's a trap we all fall into. If mini-skirts are in and they're not for you, it doesn't mean you're doomed to wear maxis. If you have thunder-thighs, just compromise – wear shorter skirts, not knicker-pelmets!

3 Check it from every angle: Does your bum look big? Can you sit down without showing your pants? Will your bra-straps show? Is it see-through? Can you walk in it? Does it squash your boobs? Is the fabric cheap and nasty? If so, don't go there!

4 If you don't love it, leave it. If you love the style but hate the colour, leave it – you'll never learn to like it. If it almost fits, leave it – you'll probably never shrink. If it's a bit too short, leeeeave it – it'll never grow.

5 What works on the catwalk won't always work in real life. Before you buy anything extraordinary, ask yourself when and where you are going to wear it. Clothes made from space-age plastic are noisy, sweaty and uncomfortable. Sky-high platforms are akin to walking with paving-slabs strapped to your feet – avoid if you live on a hill, etc., etc.

6 Don't leave without trying it on: dress sizes vary enormously from shop to shop. Most shops will exchange, but it's a wasted bus fare and you'll need the receipt.

7 Don't try and guess if the new top will match the skirt at home – if you're buying separates to go with something, bring the other item with you in a bag or wear it to the shops.

8 Don't squeeze into a size smaller in the thin hope you'll lose weight. Always buy the right size – who's gonna check the label? You'll look much better in the right fit and you can wear it now!

9 Choose colours that suit you. Some of us look fab in black – others look like the living dead. It all depends on your skin tone and hair colour. You either have yellow, pink or blue skin tones. If you're not sure, ask at the make-up counter. If you're yellow-toned, avoid yellowy colours (i.e. orange, mustard). If you're pink, strong pinks/scarlets can make you look lobstery. And if you're blue, avoid overly-blue stuff or you'll look kind of frozen!

Q My mum insists on taking me to a kids' shoe shop to get my feet measured – why does she have to show me up like this?

She does it to get you back for ruining her figure when you were born. Na, she doesn't really – if you're under 21, she does it because your feet are still growing. If you wear badly-fitting shoes now, you'll end up with corns, bunions and gross, painful trotters by the time you're her age. Go in disguise, get your feet measured, then in a calm, mature way, pick out which shoes you like.

Oooh, darling, those bows are so you!

Q Help! I've got massive feet – what shoes should I wear?

Dear Bigfoot, whatever you do, avoid white or your feet will look like ocean liners. Stick to black, brown and neutral colours.
Elongated pointy shoes and fat platties are a no-no – go for square toes. Flatties can make your foot look bigger – choose a medium heel which gives the illusion of a smaller foot.

Q Help! New shoes always rub my heels to bits at the back!

Go to the chemist, find the foot counter and look for special, heel-shaped plasters that prevent blisters. Wear them to protect your heel until your shoes soften up with wear, and never pop yer blisters – they might get infected.

Q Help – I've got short legs but I'm not allowed to wear heels to school.

If you want to make your legs look longer, tottering heels aren't the answer. They just push your feet forward, squash your toes and make you look like a short kid in big sister's shoes. The trick is to find shoes with a medium heel and a thicker sole, or shoes cut low at the front – this style makes legs look longer as if by magic.

Wow! It's easy to see who's been reading this book. They smell good. They look fit. And they dress like a dream. If that's not you yet, it could be! Try doing it one step at a time.

There are some things you can change instantly – like personal hygiene and posture. Other things take longer, like noticing the benefit of eating the right food and exercising – but you'll soon notice the difference, so keep it up.

Dress sense also develops over time. Style isn't to do with how big your clothes allowance is – it's about finding out who you are and what works best for you. So have fun – experiment!

Remember, some things that bug you about your body will get better all by themselves – you haven't finished growing yet! Of course, there are some things you just can't change. But hey, learn to love your big nose and chubby thighs. There are loads of small-nosed, weedy-thighed girls who would love to look like you! Why? Because you are the most beautiful girl in the world.

Believe it and you will be!

INDEX

Where Next? For further advice, check out:

Being Girl: www.beinggirl.co.uk

ChildLine: 0800 11 11 • www.childline.co.uk

National Drugs Helpline: 0800 002200
www.talktofrank.com